Floral Bouquets

Charlene Tarbox

To my grandmother Laura, a truly generous soul.

Note

In the present volume, artist and designer Charlene Tarbox has gathered 30 delightful floral bouquets for the coloring enthusiast. From simple nosegays of daisies and tulips to more ornate arrangements of orchids, lilies and roses, these bouquets evoke the charm and grace of fresh flowers. Whether they're contained in exquisite vases, pitchers or baskets, or simply tied together with a ribbon, these floral treasures are sure to please.

23

Beautiful Flower Arrangements

Charlene
Tarbox

To Ester Yourke
who loves beautiful things
and especially appreciates lovely gardens.

NOTE

The graceful art of flower arrangement is devoted to showing the delicate beauty of the flower in full bloom. This vibrant assortment of thirty floral arrangements includes a charming centerpiece with candles, a spray with ribbon, Asian-inspired arrangements, and exquisite bouquets in ornate vases and decorative pitchers. These elegant and finely detailed illustrations of irises, lilies, carnations, and other delightful favorites are ideal for use in any arts and crafts project. Simply add your own color to bring these images of blossoms to stunning life.

35

44

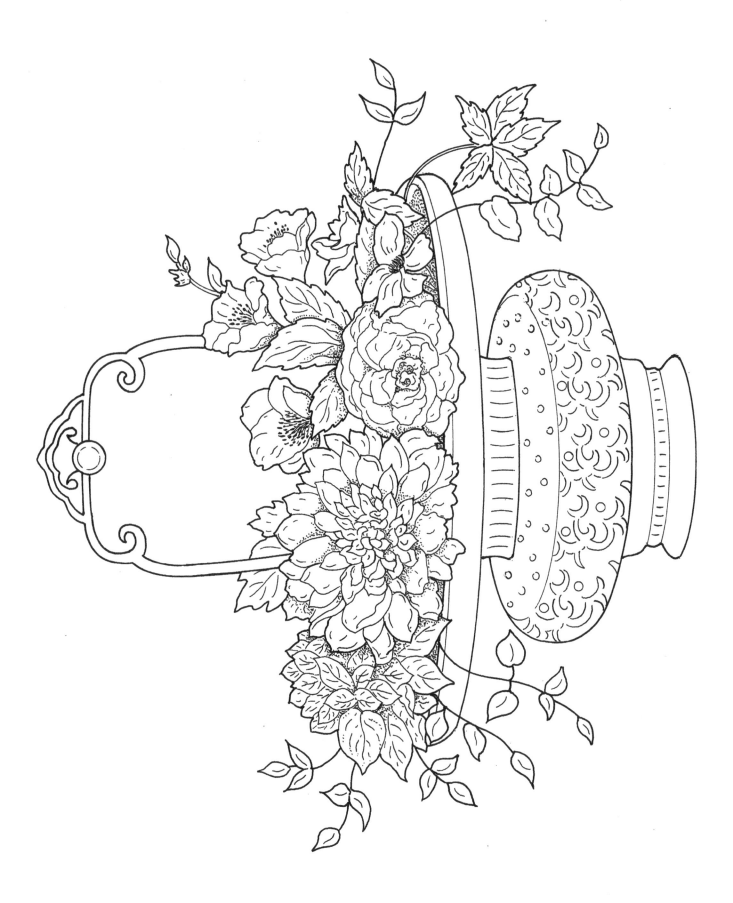

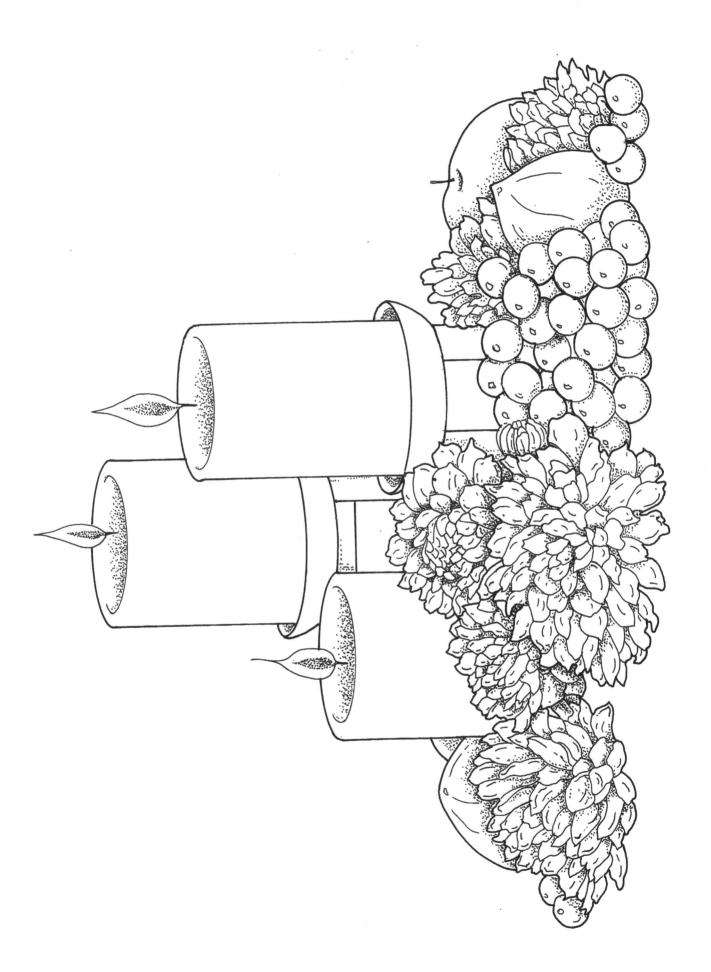

60

Redouté Flowers

COLORING BOOK

Charlene
Tarbox

NOTE

The flowers in this book are carefully rendered after paintings by Pierre-Joseph Redouté (1759–1840). In this collection of floral illustrations, one can truly appreciate Redouté's botanical artistry. Redouté, perhaps best known for his breathtaking paintings of roses, created many of his works while employed by Empress Josephine. The floral plates are arranged alphabetically according to common name. The captions also include the flower's scientific name.

Alpine Brier Rose *(Rosa pendulina vulgaris)*

Althaea, Rose-of-Sharon (*Hibiscus syriacus*)

Amaryllis *(Hippeastrum puniceum)*

Anemone (*Anemone coronaria*)

Apple Blossoms *(Malus pumila)*

Bindweed, Dwarf Morning-Glory (*Convolvulus tricolor*)

Burgundy Rose *(Rosa centifolia parvifolia)*

Campion *(Lychnis coronata)*

China Aster *(Callistephus chinensis)*

Christmas Rose and Carnations (*Helleborus niger* and *Dianthus caryophyllus*)

Dahlia *(Dahlia pinnata)*

Dillenia *(Hibbertia scandens)*

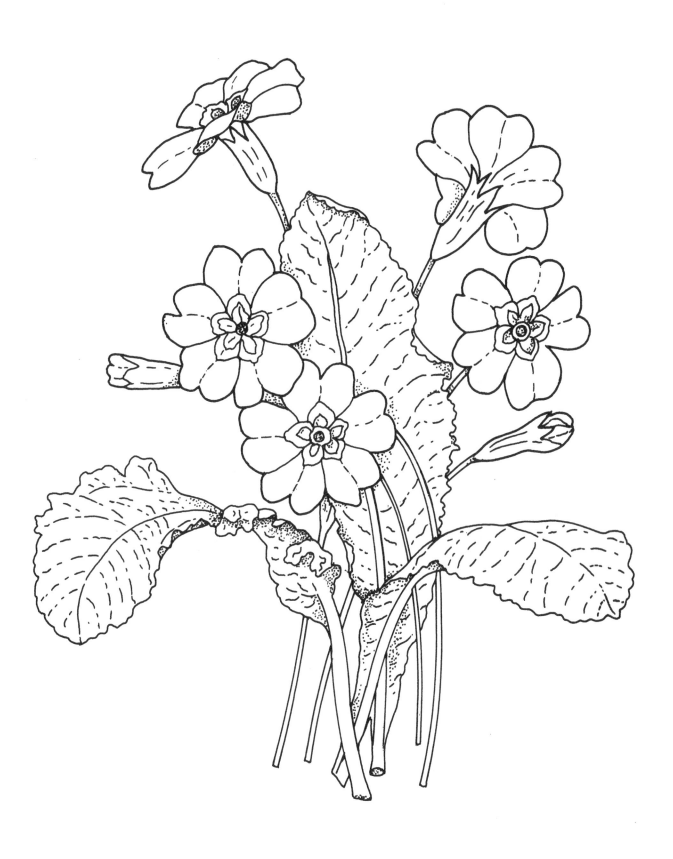

English Primrose *(Primula vulgaris)*

Enkianthus (*Enkianthus quinqueflorus*)

Gaillardia *(Gaillardia pulchella)*

Gentian *(Gentiana acaulis)*

Geranium *(Pelargonium daveyanum)*

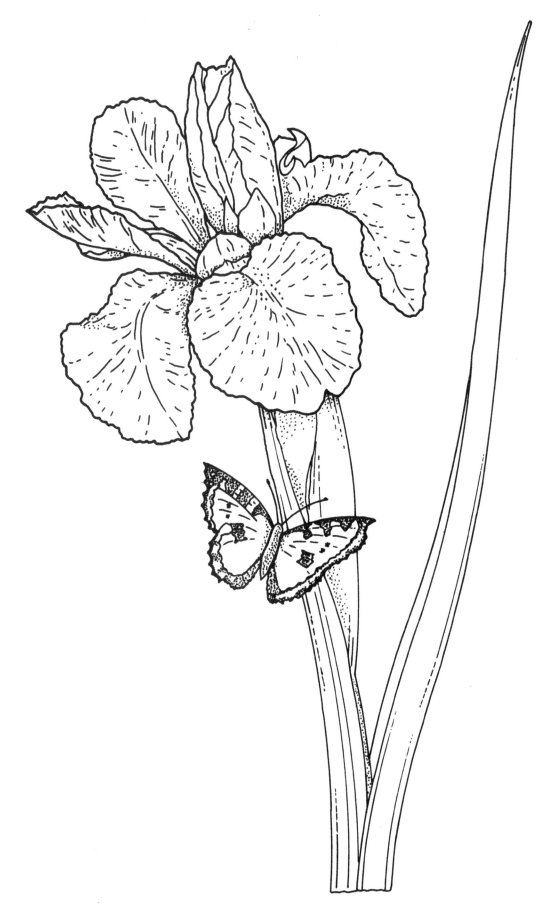

Iris *(Iris xiphium)*

Italian Damask Rose *(Rosa damascena italica)*

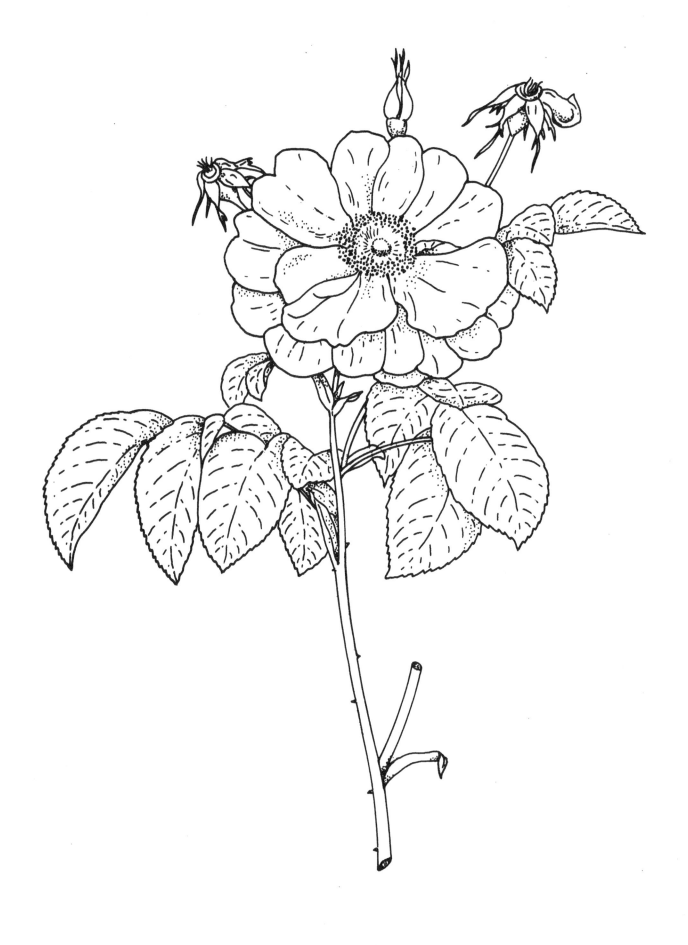

Marbled Rose (*Rosa gallica flore marmoreo*)

Narcissus / Daffodil hybrid *(Narcissus x incomparabilis)*

Peony (white form) *(Paeonia officinalis)*

Peony (deep pink form) *(Paeonia officinalis)*

Rose of Love (*Rosa gallica pumila*)

Rose of Orleans, French Rose *(Rosa gallica aurelianensis)*

Soft Rose *(Rosa mollis)*